The SPORTS HEROES Library

Football's TOUGHEST TIGHT ENDS

Nathan Aaseng

Lerner Publications Company • Minneapolis

To Doug, Jean, Carrie, and Brian

LIBRARY OF CONGRESS CATALOGING IN PUBLICATION DATA

Aaseng, Nathan.
Football's toughest tight ends.

(The Sports heroes library)
SUMMARY: Brief biographies of eight tight ends of
professional football including Ron Kramer, John Mackey,
Charlie Sanders, Raymond Chester, Dave Casper, Russ
Francis, Riley Odoms, and Ozzie Newsome.

1. Tight ends (Football)—United States—Biography—
Juvenile literature. [1. Football players]   I. Title.

GV939.A1A19   796.332'092'2 [B] [920]   80-27803
ISBN 0-8225-1070-7

Manufactured in the United States of America

International Standard Book Number: 0-8225-1070-7
Library of Congress Catalog Card Number: 80-27803

1 2 3 4 5 6 7 8 9 10 90 89 88 87 86 85 84 83 82 81

Contents

Oakland's Raymond Chester gallops down the sidelines with a
Buffalo Bill trailing behind.

4

Introduction

WANTED: *One great athlete. Must be tall and weigh about 240 pounds with all muscle, no fat. Should be extremely fast runner and nimble as a gymnast. Above-average intelligence, hard worker.*

This imaginary want ad sounds as though it is looking for someone to play the part of Superman. Actually, the ad only describes what a professional football coach looks for in a tight end. If the ad seems to describe the perfect athlete, it is no accident. The tight end has so many different jobs to do that it takes a superior athlete to play the position.

The tight end is supposed to block as well as a lineman does. And he must be large and powerful if he hopes to push around giant defensive linemen. He also must be tall in order to catch the ball even when surrounded by the defense. And unless he has a sprinter's speed, he cannot catch the long passes that are thrown to him. Often the tight end finds himself twisting and lunging for balls that are almost impossible to catch. But even then he is expected to come up with the ball. Finally, the tight end must be smart enough to figure out just how to get into the open against any one of countless defensive formations.

The position of tight end is called that because the tight end is an end, or pass receiver, who lines up close, or "tight," against the rest of the offensive linemen. (The wide ends line up by themselves toward the sidelines.)

The tight end is the only football position that started in the pro leagues instead of in college. As early as the 1930s, pro teams occasionally took one of their three running backs and lined him up next to the offensive tackle as an extra blocker.

The first large players to do well as pass receivers did not begin playing until the 1950s. Then 220-pound Pete Pihos of the Philadelphia Eagles and 6-foot, 5-inch, 260-pound Leon Hart of the Detroit Lions were catching many passes. While they were large wide receivers rather than true tight ends, they showed that players did not have to be wiry,

Dave Casper, Oakland's star tight end from 1974 to 1980, escapes a Detroit Lion tackler.

little speedsters in order to catch the football. The first modern tight end was Ron Kramer who started playing in 1957. Since his time, the tight end position has become one of the most important in the offensive line.

As an example of the importance of the tight end, many point to the rivalry between the National and American Football conferences. During the 1960s and the early 1970s, the National Football Conference (NFC) was the stronger conference. But since then, the American Football Conference (AFC) has moved ahead. In the last few years, the AFC has won over 60% of their matches and eight of the last nine Super Bowls. What has caused this shift?

A look at the contents of this book may give a clue. The first three players played in the 1960s and the early 1970s. They were the best of their time, and they all played in the NFC. The last five players have been the top stars of the 1970s. All play for AFC teams.

Perhaps this fact is merely a coincidence. But it gives good reason to think how important a tight end is to a winning team. And here is a look at eight tremendous athletes who have starred at that position.

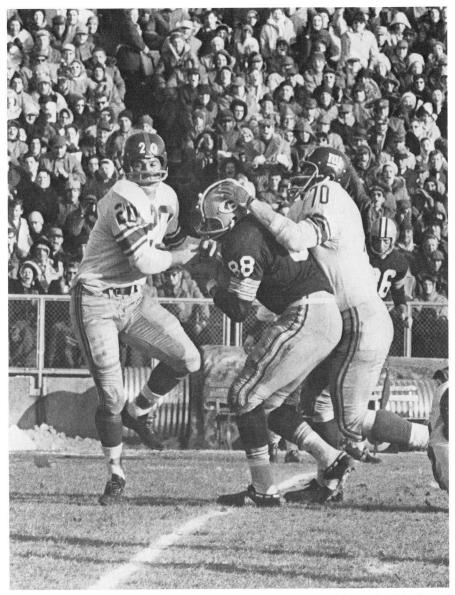

Green Bay's Ron Kramer was the first great tight end. Here he tries to break away from two New York Giants.

9

Big as a bull and strong as an ox, Ron Kramer was tough to bring down.

1
Ron Kramer

Coach Vince Lombardi did not expect to find much talent when he took charge of the Green Bay Packers in 1959. The Packers, after all, were the team that the rest of the league had pushed around the year before. But Lombardi was counting on a few fine prospects to help him. One was Ron Kramer.

Ron was a huge man with fast feet and sure hands. Before he came along, coaches had only wished for a pass receiver with all of these strengths. Because of his abilities, Kramer was the first man to show the true value of the tight end position.

Ron Kramer was born in Gerard, Kansas, in 1935, but his family later moved to Detroit,

Michigan. There he grew into an unstoppable sports star. He starred in three sports in high school, and after graduation he entered the University of Michigan.

In college most athletes only worked on their best sport. But Kramer was different. He muscled his way in close to the basket to grab rebounds in basketball. In track Ron not only used his muscles to put the shot and toss the discus, he somehow could hurl himself over the high jump bar as well. And on the football field, he could control the game all by himself. Ron was voted Michigan's Most Valuable Player all three years that he played.

The Packers eagerly snatched Kramer on the first round of the 1957 college player draft. At Green Bay, Ron started romping through defenses from the very start. In his first year, he caught 28 passes for 338 yards before breaking a leg. Ron not only had to sit out the end of that season, he also had to miss the following year. By then his leg was better, but he was drafted for the second time in two years—this time by the United States Air Force. During Kramer's absence, Green Bay had great difficulties in moving the ball.

When Ron got back into his green and gold

Kramer helped coach Vince Lombardi's Packers win the NFL title in 1961 and 1962.

Packer uniform in 1959, Packer fans expected big things from him. But they could not have been more disappointed with Kramer's performance. The talented tight end, whom the new coach Lombardi was depending on, seemed to have left his strength in the air force. Ron's legs were badly out of shape and because of his troubles, his attitude began to turn sour. Ron became moody and did not seem to have his mind on football.

Lombardi waited patiently for Kramer to snap

out of his slump. But that year, the Packer offense had to get along without any help from Ron. Then the following season, Green Bay won the Western Division title. But Ron had little to do with the win. Instead he was just filling up space on the bench.

By 1961 Lombardi was at the end of his patience. If it had not been for Ron's great reputation and raw ability, the Packers would have said goodbye to him long ago. During the exhibition season, Lombardi took Kramer aside for a chat. He told him that this would be his last chance. If he did not start playing well, Lombardi threatened, he would drop him from the team.

Kramer must have gotten Lombardi's message because he began catching passes and blocking fiercely. Linebackers were soon complaining that getting blocked by Ron was like running into a wall! On plays run to his side of the line, Ron could hold off the largest linemen. But it was the sweep around the ends that made the Packers famous. Ron's task was to handle one of the linebackers and drive him clear out of the play. Many a Green Bay runner thought his path was blocked, only to see a defender quickly disappear under a Kramer block.

Ron Kramer

With the old Ron Kramer back in action, the Packers easily won their division again. Then they faced the New York Giants in the title game. The Giants had made up their minds to stop Green Bay's tough fullback, Jim Taylor. But with the linebackers chasing after Taylor, Ron found himself roaming free in the defensive backfield. The smaller defensive backs were not used to shadowing such a large, strong man. Ron was able to grab two touchdown passes to give Green Bay a 37-0 win! In just one year, Ron Kramer had gone from a moody benchwarmer to an All-Pro.

The following season, 1962, Ron and the Packers were at their best. They had so much talent that once they even scored on one of their rare mistakes. During one game with the Chicago Bears, Packer end Max McGee was supposed to run away from Ron. That would make some of the defensive backs follow Max, and Ron would then find a less-crowded field for receiving the pass. McGee, however, made a wrong turn and led defenders straight *into* Kramer's area. Fortunately, Ron was strong enough to hold off the tacklers with a straight-arm, and he ran 56 yards for a touchdown.

Ron was again chosen All-Pro following the 1962 season. That year he had caught 37 passes for 555 yards and seven touchdowns. Even more important, he had flattened linebackers as if they were bowling pins. Grateful Packer running backs gained huge chunks of yardage, and Green Bay went into the championship game with 13 wins and only 1 loss. Although their opponent, the New York Giants, made it a closer game than they had the year before, Green Bay still won, 16-7.

Ron continued to play well for strong Packer teams until 1964. Then he was traded to his home-town team, the Detroit Lions. The 6-foot, 3-inch, 245-pound tight end kept up his fine play, but the Lions were not as successful as the Packers had been.

After four seasons with the Lions, Kramer retired to work for a steel corporation in 1968. By then everyone in the pros was searching for a tight end who could play just like Kramer. Newcomers like Mike Ditka of the Chicago Bears and John Mackey of the Baltimore Colts soon began to take over the headlines.

Ron Kramer had finished his career with two championships and many good memories. Corner-backs in football also had many memories of Kramer, but they were not as pleasant. They remembered Ron as the blueprint for the new position of tight end. His arrival on the football scene had meant that life would never be the same for the defensive backs.

Baltimore's John Mackey was a touchdown threat every time he caught the ball.

18

2
John
Mackey

Pro defenses will try almost anything to keep a tight end from getting loose in the defensive backfield. From the second the ball is hiked, linebackers are sent to badger them. Often tight ends are half tackled by the time the ball is thrown to them. They must try to get past the first down markers when going out for a pass because they know they will not get many yards after the catch.

For John Mackey, however, the largest gains came *after* he had caught the ball. Although John did not play running back in the pros, he was one of the hardest men to tackle. It did not matter whether he was being mobbed when catching the ball or while sprinting by himself across the middle of the field. Tackling Mackey was about as frightening a job as there was in the game of football.

John Mackey was born in New York City in 1941. A minister's son, he was a very quiet, serious boy. Although he was a football star at his Long Island high school, John's father did not let success go to his son's head. To help keep him humble, his father kept John busy sweeping the church floors. It worked almost too well and for a while, John rarely spoke. Only years later did people find out that John had his father's gift for speaking.

In 1959 Mackey enrolled at Syracuse University, the school of his hero, Jim Brown. At Syracuse, John was so dedicated to football and to his studies that he had time for little else. During his freshman year he met his future wife, Sylvia. While he liked her from the start, he wouldn't ask her out until after football season was over. Such dedication made him both a top end and halfback as well as a fine student.

The Baltimore Colts liked John's performance and drafted him in the first round of the 1963 college player draft. If they had expected a timid, scared rookie, they were in for a surprise. John made a name for himself as one of the first rookies to bring his lawyer with him to talk about his contract. In the years that followed, nearly every rookie followed his example.

A lineman's arms take a lot of punishment. The tape Mackey is wrapping around his arm will give him some protection.

Mackey was 6 feet, 2 inches tall and weighed 220 pounds, which was fairly light for a tight end. Most teams preferred a larger man to clear the way for the running backs, but Mackey was as solid as a rock and a hard worker, too. He was able to build up speed quickly and to level even the toughest middle linebacker. John also proved to his wide-eyed coaches that he was the fastest runner on the team. They could hardly wait to spring Mackey on unsuspecting defensive backs during the coming season.

But for all of his skill and intelligence, during his first year in the pros Mackey was fooled by some of the oldest tricks in sports. During one game John raced downfield, leaving a Los Angeles Ram defender far behind. Quarterback Johnny Unitas floated the ball towards John. It seemed like an easy touchdown but just before the ball arrived, the Ram screamed, "Look out!" John took his eye off the ball, and it bounced out of his hands.

Despite that embarrassing play, John enjoyed a fine first year. Though his total of 35 pass catches was not exceptional, his record of 726 yards gained was amazing. Even the speedy little wide receivers rarely averaged the over 20 yards per catch that John did. Mackey also pulled in seven touchdown passes and was the only rookie named to play in the Pro Bowl game that year.

Mackey soon became one of the most feared receivers in pro football for a reason other than his speed. Tackling John was like trying to knock down a runaway steer. Defensive backs actually bounced off him like beach balls. If they were

Mackey gets away from a New York Jet.

lucky, they would desperately cling to John's ankles until larger linemen and linebackers came to help them out. The way John charged while running made defenders feel he was hunting them instead of the other way around!

In 1966 Mackey was right in the middle of the

most astonishing run in modern football history. When the Colts faced the rugged defense of the Detroit Lions, the play started innocently when John caught a five-yard pass. Immediately a cornerback rushed in to make the tackle. While John was shaking him off, the rest of the defense closed in. Two tacklers grabbed John, and then another joined in. More Lions piled on, but the mass of bodies kept inching downfield. Suddenly, with half the defense struggling to bring him to a stop, John broke clear and charged downfield. He brushed off another defender, faked out another, plowed over his own teammate, and galloped 64 yards for a touchdown.

John was named All-Pro in 1966, 1967, and 1968 and played in five Pro Bowl contests. Few tight ends could match his finest year, 1966. That year Mackey caught 50 passes, gained 829 yards, and scored nine touchdowns, including an 89-yard romp. During the next few years, John was watched as closely as a lighted stick of dynamite. He once even blew past football's fiercest tackler, Chicago Bear Dick Butkus, and turned a short gain into a touchdown. While defenders worried about Mackey, the other Colts continued to run through the defense for large gains. Mackey and his teammates won the National Football League title in 1968. In the Super Bowl, however, they were embarrassed by the underdog New York Jets, 16-7.

As tough as he was, John was not indestructible. In 1970 he suffered a bad kneecap injury that put him in the hospital. John was president of the pro football players association then, and he would often spend time working for the players when he should have been exercising his knee instead.

In 1971 John put all his efforts into making a comeback in football. He won back his starting job but hurt his elbow in the third game of the year. That injury was the beginning of the end for John. He was later to complain he had not been treated fairly by pro football clubs because of his role in the 1970 player strike. But whatever the reason, the 1971 season was John's final one.

Mackey's last game was one of the most memorable in his career. With Tom Mitchell playing tight end, Baltimore had advanced to the 1972 Super Bowl. There they faced a Dallas Cowboy team that was just as determined to finally win a championship as the Colts were. Mackey was in the game for the key play. He was running his pass pattern when he saw the football sailing toward a closely guarded teammate. The ball bounced up in the air, and John grabbed it. Some of the old Mackey speed was still there, and he completed the 75-yard touchdown pass.

The Cowboys argued loudly about the play. They said the ball had been tipped by the Colt receiver. According to the rules, an offensive player could not catch a ball if it was last touched by a teammate. But a Cowboy defender, Mel Renfro, had also touched the ball, and so the score was allowed. The play, which helped the Colts to a 16-13 win, may have been the luckiest of John's career. Few players, though, were more deserving of a good break.

John had been playing pro ball for only six years when, in 1968, he had been voted the best tight end in pro history. That made it obvious to everyone that John Mackey was indeed a very special football player.

3
Charlie Sanders

If medals in football were given out for being wounded in action, Charlie Sanders would need a wheelbarrow to cart all of his home. His all-out effort on even the most dangerous of passes usually left him open to many hard hits. But the bumps and bruises did not matter to him as long as he caught the ball. And Sanders caught enough passes in his career to win a spot in the Pro Bowl game for seven of the eight years he was healthy.

Charlie Sanders was born in Greensboro, North Carolina, in 1946. North Carolina was a basketball-crazy state, and Charlie did his part at Dudley High School. He matched points with his friend Lou Hudson, who later starred in the National Basketball Association (NBA) with the Atlanta Hawks and the Los Angeles Lakers. Lou talked Charlie into following him up north to school at the University of Minnesota. But he could not talk Charlie into staying with basketball. Charlie decided that football, not basketball, would be his best chance for stardom.

Sanders' athletic ability attracted a very unusual offer. During his freshman year, 1964, he took a physical education course from the Minnesota hockey coach, John Mariucci. Charlie had never been out on the ice in his life until the class went skating. But before long he was gliding along as if he had been skating for years. The coach was so impressed that he stunned Charlie by asking him to try out for the hockey team.

Charlie, however, had his heart set on football. But the football coaches spent several years trying to find the right spot for him. As a sophomore, the 6-foot, 4-inch, 200-pounder was tried as a wide receiver. But Charlie had his troubles at that position, so he was told to try tight end. The coaches advised Charlie to put on some weight over the summer so he would be large enough to stand up to the job of tight end. So that summer Charlie drank thick banana malts as if they were glasses of water. Sanders also lifted weights and did

Charlie Sanders as a University of Minnesota student

construction work back in North Carolina. By the time school started in the fall, Sanders was 30 pounds heavier.

While 230 pounds was a good size for a tight end, it was also not a bad weight for a defensive lineman. So in 1966 Charlie found himself learning how to hold his ground as a defensive end. One year later, a change was made that helped two young men enjoy fine pro careers. Both Charlie and another defensive lineman, John Williams, were moved to the offense. Williams, later a star with the Baltimore Colts and the Los Angeles Rams, was able to clear wide paths for Minnesota runners. Then tight end Sanders knocked down anyone left standing. With Sanders and Williams on the team, Minnesota had one of their finest seasons in years.

Charlie's one year at tight end was not enough for the pros to really find out how good he was, though. So it wasn't until the third round of the 1968 college player draft that the Detroit Lions chose him. But Sanders turned out to be a bargain for his new team. He caught everything that came his way and was voted to the Pro Bowl game during his rookie season.

That year Charlie won a lot of cheers from the Lion fans, who could be very hard to please. While many athletes took great pains to be left alone, Charlie believed that a pro athlete really belonged to the fans. So he tried his best to be around when he was needed and signed autographs and gave interviews without complaining.

Sanders may have belonged to the fans when he was not playing, but during a game he seemed to loan his body to his team. Few people have ever taken the game of football as seriously as

Sanders as a Detroit Lion

Charlie did. He got himself so excited before a game that even his own teammates wanted to stay away from him. During one team meeting, Sanders had so much nervous energy that he absent-mindedly squeezed a chair until it broke! He could not force himself to eat any food from Saturday before the game until Monday, when he had finally settled down. Even when the games were over, he went through every play again in his mind.

Sanders clutches the ball after beating the Cardinals' Jerry Stovall.

Detroit quarterback Greg Landry was amazed at how well Charlie could block everything out of his mind when he went after a pass. Sanders would pay no attention to the defenders who were charging at him, ready to hit him the second the ball touched his hands. He did not seem to notice if there were linebackers hanging all over him, if the crowd was screaming, or even if the play was an important one that could decide the game. If he had to leap high in the air or sail over a defender with his body stretched out flat to catch a pass, that was exactly what he would do. Charlie even caught balls when upside down and doing cartwheels!

And best of all, Sanders made his finest catches when they counted the most. His teammates could not remember all of the times that Charlie kept an offensive drive going by grabbing an important pass on third down.

Sanders' reckless play took its toll over the years, however. After some games, Charlie would be so sore that he would limp around all the following week. Even by game time, it seemed as though he could hardly move. But as soon as the game started, Sanders was out on the field, blocking one defender and circling back to see who else he could knock down. When it was game time, Charlie always played hard.

Sanders helped the Lions earn a play-off spot against the Dallas Cowboys in 1970. That was the only play-off game Charlie ever played in, and the Lions lost, 5-0. Some people felt sorry for him because the great tight end had never been on a championship team. But Charlie had no regrets. He took pride in doing his job well, no matter what the score of the game.

In 1978 the time finally came when Sanders could no longer even limp back into the Lion huddle. The year before, he had reinjured the knee he had previously hurt in 1976. After an operation, he thought about trying to play again, but he realized his knee would no longer allow him to go full speed.

Charlie had caught 336 passes during his career, a Detroit club record. He had also caught 31 touchdown passes and had played in seven Pro Bowl games—in 1968, 1969, 1970, 1971, 1974, 1975, and 1976. When Charlie announced his retirement, his decision was typical of the way he had played. He would play the game hard, he said, or he would not play at all.

4
Raymond Chester

Raymond Chester liked to spread the credit around. He gave an entire neighborhood part of the praise for helping him to become a star tight end. Ray, born in 1948, spent his entire childhood in Baltimore, Maryland. It was a place he remembered fondly.

From his neighborhood, Raymond had learned a deep sense of teamwork. The people in his neighborhood were friendly and outgoing and watched out for each other. As Raymond began to appreciate how his neighbors helped to keep him out of trouble, he began to watch out for younger children and to use his husky build to help protect the smaller ones.

The "all-for-one" spirit of Chester's neighborhood helped to make him a valuable team player in any sport. And his large, muscular build and fine coordination did not hurt either. In addition to anchoring the football line, Raymond starred in wrestling and track at Douglas High School.

In 1966 Chester was all set to attend the University of Maryland. But a coach at Baltimore's Morgan State College offered Raymond a chance he could not turn down. The coach told Chester he could play as a tight end instead of a lineman. The glamour and excitement of pass catching helped Raymond change his mind, and he headed for Morgan State.

Raymond did so well at tight end that the coach soon wished he could have a Ray Chester at every position. In fact, when things got desperate, he could not help but try to play Chester at nearly every position. At Morgan State, Chester played all four years and broke team records for receiving.

The Oakland Raiders had had their scouts watching Chester. When they made him their number one draft choice in 1970, their admiration for Raymond quickly spread to the rest of the league. Chester stood 6 feet, 4 inches, and weighed 236 pounds, so few linebackers looked forward to an afternoon of fighting off his blocks. Just as important to the Raiders was Ray's speed. The Raiders, known as football's Mad Bombers, loved a wide open game and fired long passes from the opening kickoff to the final gun. Chester gave Oakland a third speedy target who could race downfield to catch up with one of quarterback Daryl Lamonica's throws.

Chester caught enough of these running, over-the-shoulder passes to win a spot in the Pro Bowl game during each of his first three years in the league. During these years, he burned opponents for 22 touchdowns, including strikes of 68 and 67 yards. Ray was a major reason why Oakland kept winning their conference title year after year. It seemed that Oakland could count on superstar performances from their tight end for many years.

But while the Raiders were successful in the regular season, they always came up short in the championship play-offs. They hunted desperately for whatever little edge they could find to help them gain the Super Bowl crown. In 1973 they hoped their problem would be solved by a huge, dominating defensive lineman like Bubba Smith of Baltimore. But the Colts were only willing to trade Smith if they could get Chester in return.

When Oakland agreed to the trade, it spelled

Chester takes a breather. Perhaps he is thinking of a play to help the Colts' offense next time they're on the field.

the end of the life of fame for Raymond. Back home in Baltimore with the rebuilding Colts, Chester was used mainly as a blocker. In his five years with Baltimore, he caught only half as many touchdown passes as he had in the three previous years with Oakland. Unnoticed, he often caught only one or two passes in a game for eight or nine yards each. But in spite of his record, the Colts knew how valuable Chester really was. When the ball was hiked, Raymond could charge forward with such force that he could knock his defensive

Chester running for daylight

man back several yards. This gave the Colt runners extra room to run.

Chester was especially popular with some of the younger players. Just as he had done in his childhood days, Chester watched out for the young rookies and helped them learn. He was always a hard worker, and his fine sense of humor was appreciated by his teammates.

In 1977 the Colts relied even more on Ray to come up with the long gains. That year he totaled 556 yards, including a 70-yard scoring pass. But the Colts' management was making life miserable and criticizing the coach and the players. Raymond tried to help calm things down, but he was not successful. So he was relieved when he heard that he was heading back to Oakland the following year, in exchange for wide receiver Mike Siani and a draft choice.

Back at Oakland, it appeared that the one-time superstar would be even more lost in the shuffle than he had been at Baltimore. The Raiders already had the league's top tight end, Dave Casper, as well as a solid backup in Warren Bankston. Raymond expected to spend the rest of his career sitting on the bench, and he caught only 13 passes in 1978.

Chester eludes the Vikings' Jim Marshall.

But the following summer, Casper missed training camp. Chester stepped in and played so well that Casper was hardly missed. When Casper did return, the Raiders decided that somehow they still had to make room for Raymond. It just did not make sense to have an All-Pro sitting on the bench. So the Raiders switched to a two tight end offense. This line-up gave Oakland extra blocking power on runs. And whenever the team needed a first down, they looked to one of their glue-fingered tight ends. That year the 31-year-old Chester caught 58 passes, 18 more than in his best All-Pro year! He did his best under pressure and grabbed 8 touchdown passes to lead the team.

When not running past defensive backs, Raymond enjoyed quiet hobbies. He became a fine bass player and also enjoyed gardening. Often he returned to his old neighborhood in Baltimore to see old friends. There they talked about the days when they used to stand on the street corners, singing songs. His old friends were glad to see that Raymond was finally getting his name back in the headlines and that people were again noticing their gentle giant.

5
Dave
Casper

Opposing coaches knew that Chilton High School would be tough to beat in 1969. The eastern Wisconsin school had a strong returning team. Then any hopes that other schools had of beating them went out the window when a newcomer walked onto the Chilton practice field. For Chilton it was like a millionaire finding a thousand dollar bill in the street.

The newcomer's name was Dave Casper. He had been born in Bemidji, Minnesota, and then had moved to Elgin, Illinois. There he played three years for St. Edward's Central High School. Now Dave had come to Chilton to play his senior year.

Chilton sent this 6-foot, 4-inch, 220-pound bruiser to guard one side of the field on defense, and Dave did his duty well. Chilton not only went undefeated, but no one scored a point against them during the entire season! On the few occasions that Dave and his teammates did not get a first down on offense, Dave was out there doing the punting. He used to punt barefoot until high school rules did not allow it. Still not content to be like the usual punter, he did his kicking wearing a bright red tennis shoe.

Casper enjoyed the good fortune of playing for winning teams during his entire football career. After high school, he went on to play college football with the powerful Notre Dame team. There he doubled as a defensive tackle and tight end and was voted the team captain in 1973. Notre Dame won the national championship that year, and Dave also added All-American and All-Academic honors to that prize.

Dave's luck continued when he was a second-round draft choice by the talented Oakland Raiders in 1974. His Raider teammates called him "Ghost" after a friendly cartoon ghost named Casper. But they could just as well have been describing his ghost-white appearance. The Oakland coaches were worried about Dave because he always looked so pale and tired. Sometimes he seemed so exhausted that Coach John Madden did not think he could even make it back to the huddle.

Oakland All-Pro Dave Casper trots on to the field.

Although the Raiders were worried about over-working him, they thought Dave had the raw ability to be a starter. But because they were convinced he could not stand up to the punishment of full-time action, they kept him on the bench for the first two years with the team. During that time, Casper caught only nine passes for fewer than 100 yards.

In 1976, however, the Raiders found out that looks were deceiving. They saw that even when Dave looked bushed, he could go as hard as anyone. So when Dave was put into the starting line-up for the opening game against the two-time world champion Pittsburgh Steelers, the Raiders knew they would quickly find out if he could play in the pros.

In the game, Dave surprised the Steelers by scoring the Raiders' first touchdown. But with five minutes to go in the game, Pittsburgh led, 28-14, and it seemed that Oakland would go down to defeat. Then Dave came through with another touchdown catch. Late in the game he was still going strong, and he helped his team march down-field for two more scores that finally put Oakland on top, 31-28.

Almost from that first game, Casper became an All-Pro. That same year, he caught twelve passes

Dave Casper

in a single game against New England. Casper's vise-grip catches were a major reason why Oakland swept to a 13-1 record, the best in pro football that year.

At the end of the season, the Raiders made it to the 1977 Super Bowl against the Minnesota Vikings. Dave got things rolling early for Oakland and scored the game's first touchdown. Then

Oakland went on to batter the Vikings, 33-14.

The next year, Dave came through with even more key plays. The Raiders again won their division and coasted into the play-offs. But the situation looked grim as the seconds ticked off in the first game. Baltimore was leading Oakland, 31-28, and the Raiders desperately needed a long first down. Raider quarterback Ken Stabler called a play known as "Ghost to the post." That was a pass pattern that sent Casper heading downfield at an angle toward the goal posts. When Dave looked up to catch sight of the pass, he saw it had been thrown over the wrong shoulder. Dave had to turn his head and twist while in full gallop. But somehow he pulled down the football for a 42-yard gain and a first down. The play allowed Oakland to kick a field goal which tied the game.

The contest dragged on into the sixth quarter of sudden-death play. Finally quarterback Stabler lofted another pass in Casper's direction. For anyone but Dave, it would have been a tough catch. But Dave clamped his fingers on to the ball, and Oakland had a close 37-31 win. Dave continued making key catches in the next week's game against the Denver Broncos, but his efforts were not enough. Denver won another close game, 20-17.

Dave was also a valuable blocker, especially when he lined up on the left side of the line. With Casper, huge left tackle Art Shell, and left guard Gene Upshaw side by side, the Raiders had over 800 pounds of All-Pro blocking for their runners. Although defenses knew Oakland would run behind these men, there was little they could do to stop them. And while Oakland's running backs were not as flashy as most runners, their great blocking always pushed them near the top of the league in yards gained.

Dave came as close to an automatic first down as there was in football. He rarely dropped a ball. In fact, he usually hung on to poorly thrown passes. He would dive, spin, fling out his arms, or latch onto the ball with his fingertips, whatever it took to hold on. For three years in a row, he led his team and all the tight ends in the league in catches.

Defenses became so desperate to stop Casper that they practically mugged him on the field. As soon as he would start to move, linebackers pounded and held him. In one game against Pittsburgh, the play was so rough that Dave's jersey was yanked out of his pants more than a dozen times. But no penalties were called. Oakland was only fined because Casper did not have his shirt tucked in!

Casper stretches for a pass against Tampa Bay.

Then in 1980 Oakland sent quarterback Ken Stabler to Houston in exchange for quarterback Dan Pastorini. Casper, who had grown dissatisfied with the Raider organization, had made no secret of the fact he would love to leave Oakland. In midseason he got his wish and found himself teamed up with his old quarterback when he joined Houston. The Oilers believed Casper's clutch catches would be worth the high price of two first-round draft choices. And sure enough, Dave played a key role in helping Houston to reach the play-offs that year.

In 1978 pro football officials had decided to make a rule that would protect pass receivers. The rule allowed the defenders only one bump on a receiver, and it had to occur within five yards of the line of scrimmage.

Because the defenses who had bothered Dave so much had made the rule necessary, it was sometimes called the Casper rule. That rule had opened up the passing game for all of the teams in the league. Receivers were given more freedom to race through the defensive backfield, and they started scoring more points than ever before. The Casper rule had also given defenders yet another reason to wish that Dave Casper had chosen some career other than pro football.

All-around athlete Russ Francis picks up yards for the New England Patriots.

6
Russ Francis

How many would give up a chance to play major league baseball, to ride in a rodeo, or to win an Olympic gold medal? To most people, these thrilling opportunities sound like the chances of a lifetime. But even though he probably would have been an instant star at each, Russ Francis had to turn down all of these opportunities. Because Russ was such an awesome athlete, he had his pick of practically any pro sports career. And when Russ finally decided to give up baseball, the rodeo, and the Olympics to become a tight end in pro football, no one could have been more pleased than the New England Patriots.

Russ was born in Seattle, Washington, in 1953.

He could thank his father for both his size and his athletic talent. Russ' father, Ed Francis, wrestled in the pro heavyweight ranks under the name "Gentleman Ed." The Francis family lived a more carefree life than most people, especially when they moved to Hawaii in 1959. There Russ enjoyed being around animals, and he someday hoped to be a veterinarian.

In 1970 the Francis family moved back to Oregon and bought a large farm. It was there that the stories about Russ, the super athlete, began. Many golfers spend their entire lives trying to shoot a score of 82 in 18 holes. But Francis managed that feat the first time he ever played!

In high school Russ joined the basketball team midway through his senior year. The team made it to the state tournament, and Russ won all-tournament honors.

One day in high school, Russ was fooling around with a javelin that belonged to the track team. The track coach saw him pick up the spear and playfully toss it. The javelin sailed over 150 feet. Instead of scolding him for playing with school equipment, the coach eagerly welcomed Russ to the track team. Six weeks later, Russ broke the national high school record for the javelin with a toss of more than 250 feet. Russ was so skilled, in fact, that he nearly made the United States Olympic team in 1972.

Francis did not seem to know the meaning of the phrase, "If at first you don't succeed, try, try again," because Russ always succeeded the *first* time. For instance, soon after Russ started pitching baseball in a local league, he was drafted by the Kansas City Royals. Then one day he thought he would try his hand at riding bulls and bucking broncos. Shortly after, Russ was offered a chance for a rodeo career.

But despite those offers, Francis was set on playing football instead. He enrolled at the University of Oregon in 1971 and did well at tight end when he was healthy. Unfortunately, Russ was not healthy very often, and he played in only 14 games during college. A broken ankle was partly to blame, as was a change in the coaching staff. When Russ found out just before his senior year that his coach had been fired, he left school in protest.

Most people thought Russ was making a bad mistake in leaving school. They said pro scouts would lose interest in him if he just sat around for a year. But a couple of scouts did not forget Russ. They figured that anyone with a well-muscled

Russ Francis

body who stood 6 feet, 6 inches, and weighed over 240 pounds was worth checking out.

When the scouts brought Russ out to a track to see how fast he was, Russ had forgotten to bring anything but his boots. So he ran the 40-yard dash in his bare feet! When the scouts saw his time of 4.7 seconds on the watch, they asked Russ to try again. They could not believe that such a big man could sprint so fast. So Russ ran again and matched his first time.

After his showing, the scouts did not care how little football Russ had played. They knew Russ had the strength to block, the speed to run, and the athletic skill to catch. In fact, if they were to design the perfect tight end, they could have done no better than to come up with Russ. So New England was pleased to claim him on the first round of the 1975 draft.

Francis was largely unknown to the fans when he showed up for training camp. But he soon made a name for himself. Russ seemed to actually enjoy the blocking as much as the pass-catching. In one play in the exhibition season, Russ belted a defensive lineman into two other onrushing defenders. All three of them fell to the ground, and New England scored an easy touchdown. Even top players and coaches said the Patriots' new tight end was so good that he made all of the other All-Pros look ordinary.

When Russ caught 35 passes his first year, many for long gains, it seemed as if he was on his way to breaking all records for tight ends. But even though he was showered with praise, Russ' statistics got worse instead of better. In 1976 he caught only 26 passes, and he caught just 16 the following year. Critics soon claimed that the Patriots were

Francis hauls in a pass against the Chargers.

not using Francis enough. They complained that a player of Russ' talent should be a major weapon in an offense.

In 1979 Russ got a chance to do more than apply his crunching blocks. And quarterback Steve Grogan finally started looking for the big number 81 more often. In the first half of the season, Russ caught

29 passes for five touchdowns. But in his bid to become the player everyone expected him to be, Russ was stopped by his old problem—injuries. First a back injury put him out of action. Then Russ suffered a severe concussion on a diving effort after a pass. Francis wound up with only 10 additional catches in the last eight games. And without Russ to lead both the running and passing game, New England collapsed in the final games and was beaten out of a play-off spot.

While Russ concentrated on football, he continued to do well at almost any athletic event he tried. He swam, surfed, skied, climbed mountains, and played tennis. He learned to fly an airplane in just one month. Russ also gave his father some help when his father went back into pro wrestling as a promoter. For several years, Russ teamed up with his brother in pro matches.

Russ had such a reputation as an athlete that people believed he could do just about anything. Once he happened to mention that he was planning on taking some skydiving lessons later in the year. Within a few days, the story was broadcast during a game on national television. By this time, however, the story had changed, and the audience was told that Francis was already a fine skydiver.

Francis looks over his shoulder for the pass.

And Russ had not even tried the sport yet! But as it turned out, the announcers were only a little ahead in their story. By that summer, Russ was parachuting with the greatest of ease. The Patriots, naturally, became extremely nervous when they heard about that latest Russ Francis adventure. They remembered when they nearly lost him in a motorcycle accident in 1979.

New England counts heavily on their super athlete to stay in one piece. Their team has been one of football's worst disappointments in the late 1970s. Despite a talented group of players, they have not even won a play-off game in many years. But the Patriots know that a healthy, experienced Russ Francis may well be the key to future success.

Denver's Riley Odoms scores six against San Francisco.

7
Riley Odoms

The Denver Broncos needed help in 1972. Their shopping list for the upcoming year was a long one, and it included good offensive linemen and linebackers and a young quarterback. Tight end seemed to be one of Denver's few solid positions. But when it was the Broncos' turn to choose a top player in the college draft, they threw away their shopping list. For as much as they needed help at other positions, they just could not pass up a player as talented as tight end Riley Odoms.

Riley was born in Luling, Texas, in 1950. His sports schedule was always so busy that he practically needed a secretary to keep track of all of the events. Riley was not only an All-State football player at West Oso High in Corpus Christi, Texas, he was also voted All-State in basketball. Then in the spring, things really got hectic. Odoms swung a powerful bat and played first base for the baseball team. At the same time, he was bringing home first-place ribbons for the track team in the high jump.

Sometimes baseball games were going on at the same time as the track meets. Then Riley would skip the baseball game, and one of his best friends would take over for him at first base. Riley finally quit the baseball team his senior year so his friend could play all of the time. Now his schedule was a little less crowded, so Riley could really work on his high jumping. As a senior, he reached a height of 6 feet, 9 inches and won the Texas state high school championship.

In 1968 Riley enrolled at the University of Houston, a school known for its high-powered offense in both football and basketball. Because Riley never wanted to sit out when there was a game going on, he played both sports during his freshman year. When Riley finally had to make a choice between the two sports, he chose football. He saw action as a tight end in his sophomore season and seemed to be a star of the future.

But in 1970 the junior tight end was a falling

Odoms of the University of Houston Cougars

star. Houston's senior tight end, Earl Thomas, prac-
ticed tirelessly and beat out Riley for the starting
job. The easy-going Odoms seemed to accept the
fact that he was not as good as Thomas. He stayed
on the bench most of the time and soon started
to lose interest in doing his best. One night the
Houston coaches made their usual check to see
that the players were in their rooms. They found
a few players missing, and one of them was Riley.
Because he had broken a team rule, Odoms was
dropped from the team for a short while.

Odoms rambles down the field.

Odoms, fortunately, learned from his mistake. The next season Earl Thomas was gone, playing for the Chicago Bears, and now Riley had the tight end position all to himself. And Riley wasted no time in proving he belonged as a starter, catching

45 passes for 730 yards. Odoms' eight touchdown catches were a main reason for the Houston Cougars being voted one of the country's top 20 teams for the third year in a row. After watching Riley shred his defense for an entire game, one coach had a simple comment. Riley was "too big, too strong, too fast."

That one year of success did not make Odoms a widely known star, but it did impress the pro scouts. Riley, although 6 feet, 4 inches, and 235 pounds, could move so swiftly that he could play any position on the field.

The St. Louis Cardinals, who had third choice in the draft, saw Riley as the perfect answer to their defensive troubles. They could just picture Odoms storming past blockers and tackling quarterbacks. Unfortunately, that was not the picture Odoms had in mind. He told the Cardinals he was a tight end and wanted to keep it that way. So St. Louis passed him up, and Denver made him the fifth player chosen in the entire draft.

Like most college players, Riley found he had much to learn in the pros. He found that Denver expected a good deal of blocking from him, and some of the blocking assignments were very complicated. Odoms also found the ball could be easily jarred loose when he trapped it against his chest on pass catches. Riley had to learn to grab the ball with his hands before tucking it in against his body.

Riley learned quickly enough to catch 21 passes during his rookie season. In the following year, 1973, he grabbed 43 passes and scored seven touchdowns. Odoms then took a firm hold on the starting tight end job for the rest of the 1970s. For the next seven years, Riley averaged about 40 catches a year and gained about 15 yards per catch. He also showed his all-around skill when he was used as a runner.

One of the more frightening sights for a defensive back was to see Odoms charging full speed into the open field on an end-around play. In that play, a running back followed his blockers to one side of the field and handed off to an end coming the other way. Riley averaged about nine yards per carry on those plays—twice as many yards as even the best running backs expected to average.

Because of the Broncos' weak blocking, Denver quarterbacks were especially happy to have a big target like Odoms. Under pressure from the defensive line, the quarterbacks would throw desperate passes in Riley's direction. Even when Denver won

Riley Odoms

the American Football Conference title in 1977, Riley was one of the few major weapons they had on offense. Denver relied on a strong defense to keep the game close for the offense.

But in the 1978 Super Bowl, neither the offense nor the defense had a good day. Quarterback Craig Morton was thrown down for losses before he even had a chance to look for a receiver. And Odoms had no better luck than the rest of his teammates.

On one of the few passes he caught, the ball was knocked out of his grip. The Dallas Cowboys recovered, and Denver ended up by losing the game, 27-10.

When limiting the defense to one bump against the pass receivers was put in the rule book in 1978, Riley went wild. He caught a career-high 54 passes to lead the team, and he gained 829 yards. Odoms also earned the honor of being the first Denver Bronco ever voted to the Pro Bowl game four times. That honor showed that pro defenses agreed with the rival college coach of many years ago: Riley *was* too big, too strong, and too fast!

8
Ozzie
Newsome

When Coach Paul "Bear" Bryant spoke, people listened. The crafty Bryant had won more games than any other active football coach. And his Alabama team had made a record 26 Sugar Bowl appearances and had won six national championships. In 1977 when Alabama was voted the top college team for the fourth time, Bear Bryant said that Ozzie Newsome was the finest receiver in Alabama history.

Some might wonder if Bryant had a short memory. Perhaps he had forgotten that Alabama was the school of Don Hutson. Hutson, the "Alabama Antelope" was generally considered to be the greatest end ever. He had made it to the Hall of Fame in both college and pro football, and no one had

Alabama's Paul "Bear" Bryant has coached many outstanding athletes. He called Ozzie Newsome the best receiver who ever played for him.

come close to his record of five straight pro-scoring titles. Hutson even caught 17 touchdown passes in a single season for the Green Bay Packers in 1942.

But no, Bryant had not forgotten Hutson. In fact, the Bear had played end on the same team as Hutson in Alabama back in the 1930s. So while he knew what Hutson could do, he still repeated that Newsome was better than the "all-time best." No wonder defensive backs were a bundle of nerves before they played against Newsome.

Ozzie was born in Muscle Shoals, Alabama, in 1956. His talent in football was so obvious that, starting with his freshman days at Colbert County High School, he has never lost a starting job on a team. That strong Alabama high school team ran what was called a wishbone offense. That attack did not use a tight end and rarely tried a forward pass. Instead there were three runners behind the quarterback. Wishbone offenses ran the ball so often that it was like they forgot it was legal to throw the ball! And the poor wide receiver often felt as useful as a raincoat salesman in a desert. He felt lucky if one pass was thrown him per game.

Ozzie, however, did not complain. His team was successful and won the state championship in his junior year. Newsome made certain he took advantage of those passes that did come his way, and one out of every three passes he caught in high school went for a touchdown.

Like all of the other players in this book, Ozzie proved his worth in other sports as well as in football. Although at 6 feet and 2 inches he was not particularly tall, Newsome played a rugged game of basketball. He was one of the star players on a team that included future pro basketball center, Leon Douglas, who later played for the Detroit Pistons and the Kansas City Kings.

One would think Ozzie would have been looking for a more wide-open offense in college. At a strong passing school, his pass-catching talents would have made him an instant star. But instead he chose the University of Alabama where the ground-hugging wishbone was used. Newsome had learned that even in a running offense, a patient receiver could get his chances. In fact, the threat of a top receiver would keep the defense from ganging up against the run and would make the offense almost unstoppable.

Newsome found himself in the usual position of being the youngest player on the field during his freshman year. But Coach Bryant wasted no time in turning to his only starting freshman. During a game against Florida State that year, Alabama ran into an unexpectedly stubborn defense.

Alabama could not get into the end zone and

trailed, 7-5, late in the game. With time running out, Alabama's quarterback threw a desperate pass in Ozzie's direction, and Ozzie made a spectacular catch to put his team within field goal range. Alabama's kicker came through and won the game, 8-7. Although just one year out of high school, Newsome led Alabama in pass catching in his freshman year.

The following three years were more of the same for Ozzie, only better. Newsome had already made up his mind to work on catching longer passes. He used his speed to outrun defensive backs and during college averaged over 20 yards per catch for a conference record. He led the team in receiving every year, and he finished his career with a total of over 2,000 yards gained. Alabama quarterbacks always felt safe throwing to Ozzie, even when he was well-covered by two or more defenders. They knew the pass did not even have to be a very good one for him to catch it.

Ozzie finished his senior year in good style with 36 catches for 804 yards, an average that season of over 22 yards per catch. At 230 pounds, he was large for a wide receiver, and he could add his solid blocking to Alabama's fearsome running game.

Ozzie also showed his quickness by returning punts for his team. He may have been the largest punt returner in the country, but he could dart away from tacklers and change directions as fast as a smaller man. All of these skills won him honors as an All-American wide receiver as well as the nickname, "Wizard of Oz."

Although Alabama had used Ozzie as a wide receiver, the Cleveland Browns had a slightly different plan for him. After selecting Newsome in the first round of the 1978 college draft, they trained him for the tight end position. Having Ozzie at tight end would give defenses a special problem. Ozzie was such a slippery receiver that it was as though the Browns had *three* wide receivers in the game. When Newsome lined up wide to one side or the other, opponents had to send people out to watch him. This left the middle more open for powerful Cleveland runners like Mike Pruitt.

In his rookie season, Ozzie found a quick way to get the defenses' attention. The first time he handled the ball, he galloped for a 33-yard score on an end-around play against the San Francisco 49'ers! In all he ran 13 times for 96 yards and two touchdowns, and he caught 38 passes for 589 yards and two more scores.

Newsome leaps for a pass against Cleveland's arch rival, the Pittsburgh Steelers.

The next season, Newsome showed why he was the most dangerous pass-catching tight end in football. That year he grabbed 55 passes for nine touchdowns. Defenders who tried to cover Ozzie had to leave other receivers open. Then the Browns could score in a hurry. Time and again in 1979, they would throw a long pass for a last-second or an overtime victory.

Ozzie Newsome

Newsome can be a valuable player just by show-ing up at the ballpark. And for the Cleveland Browns, Ozzie often *is* the game plan because they usually wait to see how the defense plays Ozzie before they decide on how to attack.

Experts predict that before long, fans will be watching Ozzie as closely as defenses already do. Because the youngster is already proving that ol' Bear Bryant certainly knew what he was talking about!

ACKNOWLEDGMENTS: The photographs are reproduced through the courtesy of: pp. 4, 7, 41 (Russ Reed Photo), 45, Oakland Raiders; pp. 9, 10, 15, Vernon J. Biever Photo; p. 13 Green Bay Packers, Vernon J. Biever Photo; pp. 18, 21, 23, 38, 39, Baltimore Colts; p. 29, University of Minnesota; p. 31, Detroit Lions; p. 32, Clifton Boutelle Photo; pp. 47, 50, Houston Oilers; pp. 52, 56, 58, 60, New England Patriots; pp. 62, 66, 69, Denver Broncos; p. 65, University of Houston; p. 72, University of Alabama; pp. 77, 78, Cleveland Browns, Henry M. Barr Studios, Inc.

Cover photograph: Michael Valeri

80